P9-DUD-042

CONTENTS

SESSIONS

APPENDICES

SMALL GROUP LEADERS

ENDORS

Charlie Holt brings us to the foot of the cross and the very heart of the Christian gospel. He invites us to ponder the death of Jesus for us and our own death to self in response to him. Powerful, compelling, transformative; a wonderful study for Easter or any other time.

The Rt. Rev. John W. Howe, Retired Bishop of the Diocese of Central Florida

The *Christian Life Trilogy* is masterfully written to tie in both an excellent small group curriculum and challenging daily devotions. This curriculum is a must for all churches desiring to have Jesus' life, death, and resurrection impact the way they go about their daily work and life. If you're a church who follows the traditional church calendar…it's a no brainer to let this excellent curriculum guide you through Lent, Easter, and Pentecost in a way you have never experienced before!

The Rev. Wes Sharp, Discipleship Priest, St. Peter's Episcopal Church, Lake Mary, FL

Many people write on topics of which they have little to no experience. Charlie Holt is different. He writes of evangelism as a result of growing a congregation. What he shares is the real deal!

The Rt. Rev. Jay Lambert, Bishop of the Diocese of Eau Claire

Fr. Charlie is a gifted teacher and his passion for the Scripture brings the Word alive for all. His enthusiasm for helping others grow in faith, his compassion for God's people and his deeply rooted relationship with Jesus make him an ideal person to create and share this transforming work.

The Ven. Kristi Alday, Archdeacon of the Diocese of Central Florida

Father Charlie Holt's series *The Crucified Life* offers all Christians not only a profound study of Scripture, but even more importantly a direct and practical means of applying the eternal truths of Christ's death and Resurrection to meet the challenges and frustrations of daily life.

Roni H.

EMENTS

In his series, Father Charlie Holt offers believing Christians new reflections on the sublime lessons of Christ's sacrifice for us, while at the same time offering means whereby we as individuals can apply the lessons of Calvary to our own lives. The series is an important opportunity to grow in faith by means of encouragement and meditation, especially as regards the self-examination that all Christians are called upon to do in our walk.

Martha Hoeber

I have attended many of Father Charlie's wonderful classes on the workings and the words of the LORD, and I believe there is no one more qualified nor one more driven through guidance of the Holy Spirit than Charlie Holt. For those of us who love the Bible, his ability to sort out complicated issues into meaningful and straightforward application is unparalleled.

Jim Grisham

I've been taught that a godly vision is born out of a recognized need in the people of God. Out of his passion for Christ, Charlie Holt has recognized a need in the people of God to grow together in community through a deeper understanding of Christ crucified, resurrected and ascended. The new small group series, The *Christian Life Trilogy* satisfies that need.

The Rev. James Sorvillo, Rector of the Church of the Ascension, Orlando, FL

The *Crucified Life: Seven Words from the Cross* will open your eyes to the significance and implications for your life of each and every word spoken by our Savior in His last moments on earth. What a blessing this study was for me! Taste this Spirit-led food for your Lenten experience.

Elizabeth Barber

Having already experienced The *Crucified Life: Seven Words from The Cross*, I can attest to the incredible impact of these messages from Jesus to us, as explored by Rev. Holt. The *Christian Life Trilogy* will reach into virtually every aspect of your life, ensuring that you will deepen your adoration for the Lord that loves you without end.

Laurie Mealor

ACKNOWLE

This project is offered to the glory of God for the renewal of the Church; and, with gratitude for the following people and organizations for their support and participation in this project:

Mrs. Brooke Holt
Mr. Matthew Ainsley
The Ven. Kristi Alday
The Rev. Wally Arp
The Rev. Jabriel S. Ballentine
Mr. Josh Bales
Mrs. Elizabeth Barber
Mr. Brian Bolton
Mrs. Nina Bolton
Ms. Helen Bostick
Mr. Robert Boarders
The Rev. Sarah Bronos
Mr. F. Scott Brown
Mrs. Candy Brown
Miss Lizzy Sult Case
The Rev. Sonia Sullivan Clifton
Mr. Dalas Davis
Mr. Samuel Dunaway

DGEMENTS

Mrs. Jenna Dunaway
Mr. John Gullett
Mrs. Martha Hoeber
The Rev. Canon Justin Holcomb
Mrs. Colette Ivanov
Ms. Kathy Krasnoff
Mrs. Laurie Mealor
Ms. Virginia Mooney
Mr. James Nedved
The Rev. Canon Tim Nunez
Mrs. Ada O'Neil
The Rev. Andrew Petiprin
Mr. Gordon Sims
The Rev. Jim Sorvillo
Mrs. Heather Startup
Mr. Joe Thoma
Mr. Jarda Tusek
Mrs. Sarah Tusek

Mr. David Wellday
Mr. Todd Wilson
Mrs. Sharon Wilson
Mr. Lemar Williams
Mrs. Karen Williams
Mrs. Susie Millonig
The Rev. Dane Wren
The Very Rev. Anthony Clark
St. Peter's Episcopal Church in Lake Mary, FL
The Cathedral Church of St. Luke, Orlando, FL
Allen White & Lifetogether Ministries, Inc.

FORE

WORD

The Resurrected Life

The Christian life is a series of journeys. Some journeys are taken entirely alone, guided only by the unseen presence of Christ working in our hearts and guiding our circumstances. Other journeys are taken with others—sometimes serendipitously and sometimes intentionally. This series invites us into a short-term but intentional journey with others. And this journey is an adventure well worth taking.

By embarking on this journey, you are committing to lively conversations, Bible study, and prayer. These commitments are not haphazard; they are purposeful, for Christians believe that it is through these activities that we often discover the presence of the Risen Christ. That is not to say that these activities are easy. In fact, they can (and should be) deeply challenging. But if we enter into them prayerfully and intentionally, they can lead us into deep and positive personal change. The miracle is that God uses these activities to reveal His Son and help us, amazingly, to see where and how His Son is at work in us.

Fr. Charlie Holt invites us on this journey as a gentle and thoughtful guide. He is aware of the potential hazards of small group activity as well as its joys, and offers both leaders and participants clear boundaries and open-ended possibilities. I would invite you to join him and others in this adventure!

- **The Rt. Rev. Gregory O. Brewer**
Bishop of the Episcopal Diocese of Central Florida

WELC

Welcome to *The Resurrected Life: Making All Things New.* Over the next seven weeks, you will experience the joy of life in community as you come together to listen, discuss, reflect, and grow together in your lives of faith.

When God created the world, He pronounced His creation "good," with one exception: man's being alone. Being alone was "not good," said God. We as human beings need each other. Even Jesus called 12 disciples to come alongside Him during His earthly ministry. We are designed for community, to live our lives alongside and in companionship with others. In the context of community, we connect with one another and with God in life-changing ways.

This unique small group curriculum will give you the opportunity to hear in-depth Biblical teaching and then openly discuss that teaching in your group, wrestling together with God's Word and providing mutual support as you allow your lives to be transformed by what you discover. The curriculum is designed to connect your weekly small group study with your individual daily times with God as well as what you hear in church each week, like a multifacted diamond, reflecting the many angles of God's truth.

This curriculum is centered on a DVD teaching series that explores *The Resurrected Life* and shows you how to live every day in the hope and power of Jesus' resurrection. There are **seven unique teaching sessions,** one for each lesson. In your small group, you will watch the DVD teaching together and then delve into the topic more deeply through the Scriptures and questions provided. Each Sunday, you will discover how the Scriptures and homilies you experience in church are related to the small group teaching.

COME

At the end of each session, you'll be referred to the corresponding Daily Devotions in *The Resurrected Life* book for the upcoming week. These Devotions will help you **further discover what the weekly teaching means for your life.** There's also a Scripture verse that we hope you will commit to memory and a place to record your own personal reflections.

We trust that *The Resurrected Life* curriculum will provide a positive introduction to small group community for those who are new to it, as well as a rich and rewarding experience for those who are veterans of small groups.

In all of this, our prayer is that you would **experience God** and the **truths of the Scriptures** in a **powerful new way** as you take part in this small group study.

INTRODUC

WELCOME TO *the*
RESURRECTED LIFE.

Today we begin a journey that takes us right to the heart of what it means to be a resurrected child of God. You may have just completed *The Crucified Life* series. Living a crucified life is a vital part of living the Christian life. But it's not the only part. Just as Jesus died on the cross and three days later rose from the dead, so we too must die to self (the crucified life) in order to live as a new person (the resurrected life.) A crucified life leads us to a resurrected life.

In *The Crucified Life*, we looked at what it means to be a disciple of Jesus Christ. Jesus calls each one of us to pick up our cross and follow Him. Picking up our cross involves dying daily to the flesh and to the old self. Yet, the death of our old self is not the final goal. It is the pathway to a new and abundant life in Christ! Death of one's self precedes resurrection to a new, vibrant life in God.

In the very last chapter of the Bible, in the book of Revelation, we read about God's vision for the future of His people and for the whole creation, spoken by the Lord Jesus Christ:

"And He who was seated on the throne said, "Behold, I am making all things new." (Revelation 21:5, ESV)

God's plan in Jesus is to make all things new. This is not just a vision of what will happen on the last day—it is also a vision of what the Lord has already begun to do. Notice the present tense of Jesus' words: "I am making all things new."

This "making all things new" began with the resurrection of Jesus Christ. On the day Jesus conquered death and arose from the grave, a new creation broke forth. Just as we read in the first chapter of Genesis when God said, "Let there be light," so on the Lord's Day, a new light burst forth from the tomb in resurrection power and glory. Jesus Christ is alive!

Beloved of God, God is giving you a new start and a new life in Jesus Christ. He is making all things new—including you!

As we begin this journey into the resurrected life, take note that today, Jesus is doing a new thing in your life. He is saying to you personally, "Behold, I am making all things new" for you. Are you ready for that new life? Let's begin the adventure together.

Charlie +

O God, who for our redemption gave your only-begotten Son to the death of the cross, and by his glorious resurrection delivered us from the power of our enemy: Grant us so to die daily to sin, that we may evermore live with him in the joy of his resurrection; through Jesus Christ your Son our Lord, who lives and reigns with you and the Holy Spirit, one God, now and for ever. Amen. –Book of Common Prayer (BCP) p. 222

USING *this* WORKBOOK

Tools to Help You Have a Great Small Group Experience

1 Notice the Table of Contents is divided into three sections: (1) Sessions; (2) Appendices; and (3) Small Group Leaders. Familiarize yourself with the Appendices. Some of them will be used in the sessions themselves.

2 If you are facilitating/leading or co-leading a small group, the section Small Group Leaders will offer you some hard-learned insights from the experiences of others that will encourage you and help you avoid common obstacles to effective small group leadership.

3 Use this workbook as a guide, not a straightjacket. If the group responds to the lesson in an unexpected but honest way, go with that. If you think of a better question than the next one in the lesson, ask it. Take to heart the insights included in the Frequently Asked Questions pages and the Small Group Leaders section.

4 You may find that you can't get through all the questions in a given lesson in the time you have. Look for the questions marked with an asterisk, and use those first if you're short on time.

5 Enjoy your small group experience.

6 Pray before each session—for your group members, for your time together, for wisdom and insight.

7 Read the Outline for Each Session on the next pages so that you understand how the sessions will flow.

OUTLINE *of* EACH SESSION

A typical group session for The Resurrected Life study
will include the following sections:

WEEKLY MEMORY VERSES. Each session opens with a Memory Verse that
emphasizes an important truth from the session. This is an optional exercise, but
we believe that memorizing Scripture can be a vital part of filling our minds with
God's truth for our lives. We encourage you to give this important habit a try.
The verses for our seven sessions are also listed in the appendix.

SHARE YOUR STORY. The foundation for spiritual growth is an intimate
connection with God and His family. You build that connection in part by sharing
your story with a few people who really know you and who earn your trust. This
section includes some simple questions to get you talking—letting you share
as much or as little of your story as you feel comfortable doing. Each session
typically offers you two options. You can get to know your whole group by
using the icebreaker question(s), or you may also desire to check in with one or
two group members, in between weekly sessions, for a deeper connection and
encouragement in your spiritual journey.

HEAR GOD'S STORY. In this section, you'll read the Biblical passages and
listen to teaching—in order to better understand God's story of creation and
redemption and discover how your story connects to the larger story of the
Bible. When the study directs you, you'll turn on the DVD and watch a short

teaching segment. You'll then have an opportunity to read a passage of Scripture and discuss both the teaching and the text. You'll be gleaning new insights from God's Word, and then discussing how you should live in light of these truths. We want to help you apply the insights from Scripture practically and creatively, from your heart as well as your head. At the end of the day, allowing the timeless truths from God's Word to transform our lives in Christ should be your greatest aim.

STUDY NOTES. This brief section provides additional commentary, background or insights into the passage you'll study in the *Hear God's Story* section.

CREATE A NEW STORY. God wants you to be a part of His Kingdom—to weave your story into His. That will mean change. It will require you to go His way rather than your own. This won't happen overnight, but it should happen steadily. By making small, simple choices, we can begin to change our direction. This is where the Bible's instruction to be "doers of the Word, not just hearers" (James 1:22) comes into play. Many people skip over this aspect of the Christian life because it can be frightening, difficult, relationally awkward or simply too much work for our busy schedules. But Jesus wanted all of His disciples to know Him personally, carry out His commands, and help outsiders connect with Him. This doesn't necessarily mean preaching on street corners. It could mean welcoming newcomers, hosting a short-term group in your home, or walking through this study with a friend. In this study, you'll have an opportunity to go beyond Bible study to biblical living. This section will also have a question or two that will challenge you to live out your faith by serving others, sharing your faith, and worshiping God.

FOR ADDITIONAL STUDY. If you have time and want to dig deeper into more Bible passages about the topic at hand, we've provided additional passages and questions. Your group may choose to read and prepare ahead of each meeting in order to cover more biblical material. If you prefer not to do study homework, this section will provide you with plenty to discuss within the group. These options allow individuals or the whole group to expand their study while still accommodating those who can't do homework or are new to your group. You can discuss this in your group or just study it on your own, whatever your group prefers.

DAILY DEVOTIONS. Each week under the heading Daily Devotions, we refer you to the Daily Devotions found in *The Resurrected Life* companion book. There is much more to learn and consider in the *The Resurrected Life book*, material that is not covered in the small group material. We encourage you to set aside a time each day for these devotions. The practice will give you a chance to slow down, delve more deeply into the weekly teaching and pray through it. Use this time to seek God on your own throughout the week. Try not to rush; take the time to truly ponder God's Word and listen for His direction.

MAKING ALL THINGS NEW

ALL THINGS NEW

Overcoming Doubt and Fear

He who was seated on the throne said, "I am making everything new!" Then He said, "Write this down, for these words are trustworthy and true."

REVELATION 21:5

After soberly contemplating our fallenness and the gift of Christ's sacrifice for us during Lent, we now enter a season of celebration: Easter. This study, *The Resurrected Life*, invites us to make a commitment to a new and abundant life in the risen Christ.

In his *Confessions*, St. Augustine wrote, "And He departed from our sight that we might return to our heart, and there find Him. For He departed, and behold, He is here." The focus of this study is on Christ's continued work—in and through us—to "make all things new."

In each of the following seven study sessions, we will reflect on the presence of Christ as we are made new in Him.

In our first session, *All Things New*, we will explore:

-   How Christ revealed His presence to His disciples and how He reveals Himself to us today.

-   Ways to address—honestly and with compassion—the doubts we or others may have.

-   The blessings Christ has promised to those who believe.

In this session, we will look at ways we can more closely follow Christ. And we'll do it the best way possible—together.

SHARE *your* STORY

Each of us has a story. The events of our lives—good, bad, wonderful, or challenging—have shaped who we are. God knows your story and He intends to redeem it, to use every struggle and every joy to ultimately bring you to Himself. When we share our stories with others, we give them the opportunity to see God at work.

When we share our stories, we also realize that we are not alone and that we have common experiences and thoughts others can understand. Others can empathize with what we are going through. Your story also can encourage someone else as you tell it, even as sharing openly becomes a path to freedom for you.

Open your group with prayer. This should be a brief, simple prayer in which you invite God to be with you as you meet. You can pray for specific requests at the end of the meeting or stop momentarily to pray if a particular situation comes up during your discussion.

If you prefer, you could use a collect from the *Book of Common Prayer* to begin your time together, such as:

O God, who dost manifest in thy servants the signs of thy presence: Send forth upon us the Spirit of love, that in companionship with one another, thine abounding grace may increase among us; through Jesus Christ our Lord. Amen. (BCP, p. 71)

As you begin, pass around a copy of the *Small Group Roster* on page 146, a sheet of paper, or one of your Study Guides opened to the *Small Group Roster*. Have everyone write down his or her contact information. Ask someone to make copies or type up a list with everyone's information and email it to the group during the week.

Ask everyone to introduce themselves. Then, begin your time together by using the following questions and activities to get people talking.

READ ACTS 4:33-34

"With great power the apostles continued to testify to the resurrection of the Lord Jesus. And God's grace was so powerfully at work in them all that there were no needy persons among them."

1. *What brought you here? What do you hope to get out of this group?

2. Growing up, were you taught to think of Easter as a *day* or as a *season*? In what ways, if any, has your perception or your celebration of Easter changed over the years?

3. Did you just attend Easter Services or even an Easter Vigil? If so, what was the experience like for you?

4. *In what ways have you seen others "testify" to the resurrection by the way they live or by sharing their faith? How is declaring "Alleluia, Christ is risen! The Lord is risen indeed. Alleluia!" a way of "testifying" to the resurrection?

5. *Whether your group is new or ongoing, it's always important to reflect on and review your values together. On pages 140 is a *Small Group Agreement* with the values we've found most useful in sustaining healthy, balanced groups. We recommend that you choose one or two values—ones you haven't previously focused on or have room to grow in—to emphasize during this study. Choose ones that will take your group to the next stage of intimacy and spiritual health.

- If your group is new, welcome newcomers. You may even want to have nametags for your first meeting.

- We recommend that you rotate host homes on a regular basis and let the hosts lead the meeting. Studies show that healthy groups rotate leadership. This helps to develop every member's ability to shepherd a few people in a safe environment. Even Jesus gave others the opportunity to serve alongside Him (Mark 6:30–44). Look at the FAQs in the Appendix for additional information about hosting or leading the group.

- The *Small Group Calendar* on page 142 is a tool for planning who will host and lead each meeting. Take a few minutes to plan hosts and leaders for your remaining meetings. Don't skip this important step! It will revolutionize your group.

OVERCOMING

WATCH *now*

DVD SESSION ONE

Jesus makes all things new

Jesus sent his priests out
into the world to preach peace.

We all have doubts. Jesus
knows what our individual
doubts are and knows what
we need to overcome the doubts

pg 316 prayer book

Watch the DVD for this session now. Use the space provided below to record any key thoughts, questions, or things you want to remember or follow up on.

After watching the video, have someone read the discussion questions in the *Hear God's Story* section and direct the discussion among the group. As you go through each of the subsequent sections, ask someone else to read the questions and rotate who directs the discussion.

HEAR *God's* STORY

Read Psalm 29:11

"The Lord gives strength to his people; the Lord blesses his people with peace."

1. *In the DVD, Fr. Charlie points out that Christ uses the present tense when He says, "I am making all things new." When you look at your family, church community, and the wider world, in what ways do you see Christ at work making things new?

God uses stories to guide us. When we read the true stories of Scripture, we learn what God is like and we see His plan unfolding. We also learn principles for our own lives. How can we become a part of God's story? By aligning our stories with His. By not just understanding what it means to follow Him, but actually doing it—changing our attitudes and actions to live as He would have us. Use the following questions to guide your discussion of the teaching and stories you just experienced, as well as the Bible passage below. You may want to use the study notes on page 31 to guide your reading and discussion.

2. How do you reconcile your faith in Christ's words (that He *is* making things new) with the brokenness you see in the world?

3. *When have you gone through times of doubt? Have they emerged during or after difficult or traumatic events? Or at particular times of transition in your life?

4. *In the teaching, Fr. Charlie said that the peace Christ offered His disciples gave them power and freedom from fear. They no longer hid together, but were able to go out into the world and be courageous. In what ways do you act with more confidence when your fear is replaced by peace? When have you witnessed this in others?

5. Where do you see a need for Christ's peace in our world today?

....

....

....

....

....

....

....

....

....

....

....

....

....

....

....

....

....

....

....

STUDY

NOTES

CHRIST'S PRESENCE. The Bible promises that Christ's presence is just as real today as it was when He appeared to the disciples after His resurrection. Share moments in your life when you have been aware of Jesus' presence.

TAKING OUR DOUBTS TO CHRIST. In the teaching, Fr. Charlie shared about a time in his life when he had profound doubts about God's existence. On the DVD, he asked us to be authentic with ourselves and each other as we acknowledge our doubts and name the parts of our faith that we feel are lacking. What do you need most from Christ today? Freedom from fear and doubt? An awareness of His presence?

CREATE *a* NEW STORY

God wants you to be a part of His Kingdom and for your story to reflect His love and power. That will mean change—choosing to go His way rather than your own. How does this change take place? Usually not overnight, but gradually and steadily. By starting with small, simple choices, we begin to change our direction. The Holy Spirit helps us along the way by giving us gifts to serve the body, offering us insights into Scripture, and challenging us to love not only those who also believe but also those who are far from God.

In this section, talk about how you will apply the wisdom you've learned from the teaching and Bible study to your life. Think about practical steps you can take in the coming week to live out what you've learned by discussing these questions:

1. Because we know that we are all doubters and skeptics from time to time, how can you be a present and compassionate listener this week to someone who is struggling with his or her faith?

2. *Name three things (people, situations, memories) in your life that fill you with dread or fear. Remember Fr. Charlie's invitation to take these to Christ and to begin to be transformed, as Thomas was, from doubter to worshipper.

3. Can you identify anyone—in your small group or elsewhere—in whom you can see the light of Christ? How so?

4. *Is there a situation this week that you can handle differently from the way you have in the past, now that you're aware that Christ is working through you?

5. *To close your time together, spend some time worshiping God by praying, singing, or reading Scripture. Here are some ideas:

- Have someone use their musical gifts to lead the group in a worship song. Try singing a cappella, using a worship CD, or having someone accompany your singing with a musical instrument.

- Choose a psalm or other favorite verse and read it aloud together. Make it a time of praise and worship as the words remind you of all God has done for you.

- Ask," How can we pray for you this week?" Invite everyone to share, but don't force the issue. Be sure to write prayer requests on your *Prayer and Praise Report* on page 144.

- Close your meeting with prayer.

for **ADDITIONAL STUDY**

If you feel God nudging you to go deeper, take some time between now and the next meeting to dig into His Word. Explore the Bible passages related to this session's theme on your own, jotting your reflections in a journal or in this study guide. A great way to gain insight into a passage is to read it in several different translations. You may want to use a Bible app or website to compare translations.

READ LUKE 24:38

"He said to them, 'Why are you troubled, and why do doubts rise in your minds?'"

Christ promises blessing to those who believe, even when—or maybe especially when—they do not "see." What does this "inability to see" look like in you? When have you had a "dark night of the soul" in which you could not see Christ at work in you or in the world? What doubts or unbelief can you lay at the cross this week?

READ EPHESIANS 1:3

"Praise be to the God and Father of our Lord Jesus Christ, who has blessed us in the heavenly realms with every spiritual blessing in Christ."

What comes to mind when you try to define or describe "spiritual blessings?" Are there any parts of your life you enjoy that you can loose or let go of that will help you worship Christ more fully? Deep down, which spiritual blessing do you most desire?

extra notes

DAILY
DEVOTIONS

Remember to set aside time each day to read the Daily Devotion found in *The Resurrected Life* book. There are seven Daily Devotions each week, one for each day, including the day your small group meets. These devotions will help you delve more deeply into this week's teaching. Listen to what God wants to say to you through His Word, and respond to Him as you meditate on the truths of Scripture.

....

....

....

....

....

....

....

....

....

....

....

....

....

....

....

....

....

....

NEW LIFE

Letting Go and Letting God

"We were therefore buried with Him through baptism into death in order that, just as Christ was raised from the dead through the glory of the Father, we too may live a new life."

ROMANS 6:4

When Mary Magdalene first interacted with the resurrected Christ, He told her not to "cling to" Him. Should we infer that Jesus' new, post-resurrection body was somehow not meant or able to be handled? No, not after we've read how Christ invited Thomas—the doubter—to touch His body, giving Thomas the evidence he needed to believe.

This week we will examine what Jesus may have meant when He admonished Mary not to cling to Him. The resurrection, Fr. Charlie reminds us, "changes everything," including the way Jesus related to the people He knew, even Thomas and Mary.

This week, we'll consider:

- In what ways do we cling to old patterns and sins, even after receiving the Light of Christ?

- What will it mean to us to live as people who have been healed?

- What might an abundant life in Christ look like for us?

Like Mary, we are invited to a new relationship with Christ. Together, we'll explore what this relationship looks and feels like.

SHARE *your* STORY

As we mentioned last week, when we tell our stories and share them with others, we give others the opportunity to see God at work in our lives and find that we are not alone. Your story is being shaped even in this moment by being a part of this group. In fact, few things can shape us more than community.

When we share our stories, we can encourage someone else, and learn. We can experience the presence of God as He helps us to be brave enough to reveal our thoughts and feelings.

Open your group with prayer. This should be a brief, simple prayer in which you invite God to guide you as you meet, to give you insight and wisdom. You can pray for specific requests at the end of the meeting, or stop momentarily to pray if a particular situation comes up during your discussion.

If you prefer, you can use this prayer from the *Book of Common Prayer* (p. 125):

O God, you manifest in your servants the signs of your presence: Send forth upon us the Spirit of love, that in companionship with one another, your abounding grace may increase among us; through Jesus Christ our Lord. Amen.

Then, begin your time together by using the following questions and activities to get people talking:

1. When you consider this part of the resurrection story, in what ways do you identify with Mary Magdalene? What might she have been feeling, physically and emotionally, before she met the risen Christ?

2. What kinds of situations make people "clingy?" Have you ever wanted to cling to someone out of fear or uncertainty?

extra NOTES

WATCH *now*

DVD SESSION TWO

Watch the DVD for this session now. Use the *Notes* space provided below to record any key thoughts, questions, or things you want to remember or follow up on. After watching the video, discuss the questions in the *Hear God's Story* section.

HEAR *God's* STORY

READ JOHN 5:7-9

"'Sir,' the invalid replied, 'I have no one to help me into the pool when the water is stirred. While I am trying to get in, someone else goes down ahead of me.'

Then Jesus said to him, 'Get up! Pick up your mat and walk.' At once the man was cured; he picked up his mat and walked."

How can we become a part of God's story? By aligning our stories with His. By understanding what it means to follow Him. Use the following questions to guide your discussion of the teaching and stories you just experienced, as well as the Bible passage on this page.

1. Fr. Charlie pointed out that, like the man who explains to Jesus that he cannot be healed because there is no one to help him get into the pool, we often believe that the options for our healing are limited. Jesus, however, has new ways of healing us. Tell about a time God healed you or someone you know in an unexpected or surprising way.

2. Can you identify any superstitious ideas or formulaic expectations that you cling to regarding how God might answer your prayers? Remember that Jesus didn't carry the man into the water when it stirred, but simply told him he could get up and walk.

3. When the man by the pool picked up his mat and walked, Fr. Charlie points out, his whole life was changed. People no longer had to carry him from place to place. He had agency, more social power, and a completely new life. How might your life change if you receive Christ's healing and resurrected life?

STUDY

NOTES

RESISTANCE TO HEALING. In his teaching, Fr. Charlie said that other people sometimes resist the changes they see in us when we have grabbed hold of healing and our lives are being transformed. Change is hard for other people; they might want us to remain as we were before. They did not feel judged when they shared certain experiences with us in which we no longer choose to engage. We, too, can hold onto stubbornness and fail to let go of our "old selves," even after we experience God's forgiveness and healing.

LIVING AS A HEALED PERSON. Fr. Charlie said that as we continue to connect to Christ, like a vine is connected to branches and receives nourishment from them, we will experience deepened life in Him. It is Jesus' will that we experience new and abundant life in Him so that we may let go of the past, of the sins that hold us back, and of our old selves.

CREATE *a* NEW STORY

In this section, talk about how you will apply the wisdom you've learned from the teaching and Bible study. Then think about practical steps you can take in the coming week to live out what you've learned. Use these questions to lead you:

4. *Has anyone ever said, "Hey, what's happened to you?" after you've made a life change? What did they see in you?

5. Where do you encounter the most resistance from others or yourself to your living fully as resurrected person in the Lord?

6. *In the DVD, Fr. Charlie recalls that some of the ways Mary Magdalene had related to Christ before His crucifixion involved clinging to Him, such as pouring oil on His feet and wiping them with her hair. He asks her to relate to Him in a new way now that He is resurrected. Consider ways that Christ might be calling you to relate in new ways to Him this week. How might you make different choices? How might you invest more in your spiritual life?

7. From the parts of Scripture we've discussed this week, to which person do you most relate? Mary? The man at the pool, longing for healing? Why?

8. *This week, look at the people around you in your small group as well as in your family (or others you know), and focus on how God is working in their lives. How can you affirm the presence of the Holy Spirit in them?

9. Take a look at the *Circles of Life* diagram below and write the names of two or three people you know who don't know about the abundant new life Christ offers. Commit to praying for God's guidance and an opportunity to share with each of them. Share your lists with the group so that you can all be praying for the people you've identified.

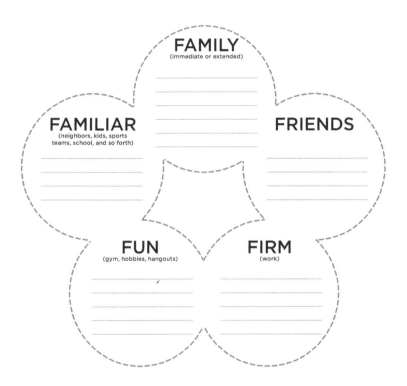

10. Developing our ability to serve according to the leading of the Holy Spirit takes time and persistence in getting to know our Lord. So the first step in serving others is, paradoxically, spending time alone with God—praying, studying, and reflecting on God's Word. Here are some simple ways to connect with God. Tell the group which one you plan to try this week, and then talk about your progress and challenges next time you meet.

- **Prayer.** Commit to personal prayer and daily connection with God. You may find it helpful to write your prayers in a journal.

- **Daily Devotions.** The Daily Devotions provided in *The Resurrected Life* book offer an opportunity to read a short Bible passage each day during the course of this study and to learn more about the topic. In our hurry-up world, we often move too quickly through everything—even reading God's Word! Slow down. Don't just skim, but take time to read carefully and reflect on the passage. You may want to journal your insights into what you read each day.

11. *To close your time together, spend some time worshiping God by praying, singing, or reading Scripture. Try an idea that you didn't try last week:

- Have someone use their musical gifts to lead the group in a worship song. Try singing along with a worship CD, a cappella, or with someone accompanying your singing with an instrument.

- Choose a psalm or other favorite verse and read it aloud together. Make it a time of praise and worship, as the words remind you of all God is teaching you.

- Ask, "How can we pray for you this week?" Invite everyone to share, but don't force the issue. Be sure to write prayer requests on your Prayer and Praise Report on page 144.

- Close your meeting with prayer.

for ADDITIONAL STUDY

If you feel God nudging you to go deeper, take some time between now and your next meeting to dig into His Word. Explore the Bible passages below on your own, jotting your reflections in a journal or in this study guide. Want to enrich your study further? Select a few verses and try paraphrasing them: writing them in your own words. If you like, share them with the group the next time you meet.

READ 2 CORINTHIANS 5:17

"Therefore, if anyone is in Christ, the new creation has come: The old has gone, the new is here!"

What are some ways you can put your "old self" behind, rejoicing in Easter's gift of new and abundant life in Christ?

In what ways do you remain "in Christ"? What do those words mean to you? Can you think of spiritually rich times in your life? What, if anything, did they have in common?

READ MATTHEW 9:22

"Jesus turned and saw her. 'Take heart, daughter,' he said, 'your faith has healed you.' And the woman was healed at that moment."

What is your gut reaction to these verses? In your experience, has healing of any kind been instantaneous or does it take time? Think of a burden you currently bear and picture Christ saying, "Take heart, daughter" or "Take heart, son." What does that feel like?

extra notes

DAILY
DEVOTIONS

Use the Daily Devotions in *The Resurrected Life* book to further explore this week's topic. Read the devotional reflection each day and take time to think through the questions at the end. Ask God to speak to you through His Word and to transform your life by His love and mercy.

....

....

....

....

....

....

....

....

....

....

....

....

....

....

....

....

....

NEW TEMPLE

Inviting God's Presence

"Do you not know that your bodies are temples of the Holy Spirit, who is in you, whom you have received from God? You are not your own; you were bought at a price. Therefore honor God with your bodies."

1 CORINTHIANS 6:19-20

Most of us have heard the mysterious teaching that our bodies are "temples of the Lord." In this session of *The Resurrected Life*, we will explore what this might mean.

We'll examine Christ's statement that He is the "cornerstone" (Matthew 21:42), words that echo the prophesy in Isaiah in which God promises that He has set a cornerstone and those who lean on it (Him) will not "be stricken with panic." (Isaiah 28:16)

In this week's study, we will delve into the idea of Christ as cornerstone, and how we as a church were created to be a new, unified temple that brings living water to a parched world.

SHARE *your* STORY

Open your group with prayer. This should be a brief, simple prayer, in which you invite God to be with you as you meet. You can pray for specific requests at the end of the meeting, or stop momentarily to pray if a particular situation comes up during your discussion.

You may also pray this collect from the *Book of Common Prayer* (BCP, p. 230)

Almighty God, you have built your Church upon the foundation of the apostles and prophets, Jesus Christ himself being the chief cornerstone: Grant us so to be joined together in unity of spirit by their teaching, that we may be made a holy temple acceptable to you; through Jesus Christ our Lord, who lives and reigns with you and the Holy Spirit, one God, for ever and ever. Amen.

Telling our personal stories builds deeper connections among group members. Begin your time together by using the following questions and activities to get people talking:

1. Why do you think the Bible employs the metaphor of a temple to describe believers? What characteristics do people and temples share?

2. When have you ever seen an old building's "cornerstone?" What does that word mean to you? In what ways might Christ be a cornerstone in our lives?

extra NOTES

WATCH *now*

DVD SESSION THREE

Watch the DVD for this session now. Use the *Notes* space provided below to record any key thoughts, questions, or things that you want to remember or ask a question about later.

HEAR *God's* STORY

READ LUKE 6:47-49

"As for everyone who comes to me and hears my words and puts them into practice, I will show you what they are like.
They are like a man building a house, who dug down deep and laid the foundation on rock. When a flood came, the torrent struck that house but could not shake it, because it was well built. But the one who hears my words and does not put them into practice is like a man who built a house on the ground without a foundation. The moment the torrent struck that house, it collapsed and its destruction was complete."

Use the following questions to guide your discussion of the DVD teaching you just experienced and the Bible passage below.

1. *What exposure have you had to the building of a house? When you hear that a house has been "well built," what sort of attributes come to mind?

2. *How have you seen collapse and destruction in life due to weak spiritual foundations?

3. Notice that those who built on a strong foundation are not spared floods, but can withstand them. What does that mean to you?

4. *What are some ways people put God's words "into practice"?

extra notes

STUDY

NOTES

CORNERSTONE. Dictionary definitions of "cornerstone" include:

- Something that is essential, indispensable, or basic

- The chief foundation on which something is constructed or developed

SANCTITY OF THE TEMPLE. The Lord calls us to be a Holy Temple in which his presence is pleased to dwell. Like the Temple of the Old Testament, our lives are to be a place where the Glory of God dwells. This means that our lives should reflect the holiness of the Lord's presence.

UNITY OF THE TEMPLE. Fr. Charlie noted that St. Paul was most outspoken in his letters when he wrote about divisions in the church. Because the church is the temple of the Holy Spirit and is a metaphor for and physical sign of Christ's presence, when we bicker and are at odds with each other within the church, we fail to fulfill Christ's purpose for us—to be "one" in Him, pointing a broken world to the true source of life and salvation, Christ Himself.

CREATE *a* NEW STORY

God wants you to be a part of His Kingdom—to find your story within His. That will mean change. It will require you to go His way rather than your own. This won't happen overnight, but it should happen steadily. By making small, simple choices, we can begin to change our direction. The Holy Spirit helps us along the way by giving us gifts to serve the body, offering us insights into Scripture, and challenging us to love not only those in the family of faith, but those far from God as well.

In this section, talk about how you will apply the wisdom you've learned in this session, using these questions:

5. *On the DVD, Fr. Charlie says that Christian unity is "absolutely essential" to the fulfillment of Christ's purposes. In what ways can you and your small group promote and nurture unity among believers?

6. *If in His deepest heart, God wants believers to worship Him "rightly," as Jesus said to the woman at the well, "in Spirit and in Truth," what does this look like for you? Your small group? Your faith community? What would worship that isn't "right" look like?

7. *Fr. Charlie ended the teaching by referring to Christians as those who are a source of living water—love, joy, grace—in the world. In what ways can your own life be a source of living water to others? What opportunities do you have in the coming week to address the physical and spiritual thirst of those around you?

8. Spend some time praying about those you know who might respond to a simple invitation to come to a church service, to join your small group, or even to just have coffee and talk about spiritual matters. Ask the Holy Spirit to bring to mind people for whom you can pray.

9. What specific steps will you take this week to cultivate your personal relationship with God? If you've focused on prayer in past weeks, maybe you'll want to direct your attention to Scripture this week. If you've been reading God's Word consistently, perhaps you'll want to take it deeper and try memorizing a verse. Tell the group which one you plan to try this week, and then, at your next meeting, talk about your progress and challenges.

10. In the last session, we asked you to write some names in the *Circles of Life* diagram. Who did you identify as the people in your life who need to meet Jesus? Go back to the *Circles of Life* diagram on page 49 to help you think of the various people you come in contact with on a regular basis, people who need to know Jesus more deeply. Consider the following ideas for action and make a plan to follow through on one of them this week:

- This is a wonderful time to welcome a few friends into your group. Which of the people you listed could you invite? It's possible that you may need to help your friend overcome obstacles to coming to a place where he or she can encounter Jesus. Does your friend need a ride to the group? Help with childcare?

- Consider inviting a friend to attend a weekend service with you and possibly plan to enjoy a meal together afterward. This can be a great opportunity to talk with someone about your faith in Jesus.

- Is there someone whom you wouldn't invite to your group but who still needs a connection? Would you be willing to have lunch or coffee with that person, catch up on life, and share something you've learned from this study? Jesus doesn't call all of us to lead small groups, but He does call every disciple to spiritually multiply his or her life of faith over time.

- Groups that connect outside of the regular meeting time build stronger bonds and feel a greater sense of purpose. Why not plan a social outing with group members? As a group, brainstorm about ways that you could do something fun together—enjoy a meal or a night out together.

11. To close your time, spend some time worshiping God together—praying, singing, reading Scripture, as you've done in previous weeks.

- Close your meeting with prayer. Be sure to write prayer requests on your *Prayer and Praise Report* on page 144.

extra NOTES

for ADDITIONAL STUDY

Take some time between now and our next meeting to delve into God's Word. Explore the Bible passages related to this session's theme on your own, jotting your reflections in a journal or in this study guide. You may even want to use a Bible website or app to look up commentary on these passages. If you like, share what you learn with the group the next time you meet.

READ JOHN 7:38

"Whoever believes in me, as Scripture has said, rivers of living water will flow from within them."

What images come to mind when you read the words "rivers of living water"? What parts of your community or world seem dried out or parched? How might you be uniquely gifted to bring water and health to these dry patches? How might you be poised to restore dried-up places in your family, neighborhood, workplace, or world?

READ GALATIANS 5:22-23

"But the fruit of the Spirit is love, joy, peace, forbearance, kindness, goodness, faithfulness, gentleness and self-control. Against such things there is no law."

If the Holy Spirit lives within us and the qualities that sprout and bloom from people who are filled with the Holy Spirit are the ones listed in the verse above, take a few minutes to consider in what ways your own life, the life of a spouse or close friend, or even the life of someone you admire from afar in your church community or elsewhere, exhibits these qualities. Which "fruit of the Spirit" is most strongly present in you?

extra notes

DAILY
DEVOTIONS

As you've done in previous weeks, read each day's Daily Devotion in *The Resurrected Life* companion book. Hopefully, this devotional time is becoming a regular part of your day. God promises to be present with us as we take time to pray and study His Word. This week, why not pray before your devotional time, asking God to lead you and guide your thoughts as you reflect on the teaching.

....

....

....

....

....

....

....

....

....

....

....

....

....

....

....

....

....

....

....

SESSION FOUR ▌▌

NEW BODY

Manifesting Jesus

"I eagerly expect and hope that I will in no way be ashamed, but will have sufficient courage so that now as always Christ will be exalted in my body, whether by life or by death."

PHILIPPIANS 1:20

In this session of *The Resurrected Life*, we will explore the truth that Christ not only cares about our *spiritual* selves, but about our *physical* bodies too.

Our physical bodies might seem like a mundane topic, given our discussions over the past few weeks about deeper, more traditionally spiritual matters, such as the Holy Spirit's ongoing work in and through us. But Jesus deeply cares about the way we care for our bodies, and when we use them well, we glorify God.

Throughout the Scriptures, the right and good uses of the physical body are detailed. We're given guidelines for what to eat and how our bodies

should come into contact with other people's bodies. What's more, the church itself is described as a "body with many parts" (1 Corinthians 12:12); our church bodies are manifestations of Christ's presence.

This week, be prepared to see your physical self for the wonderful gift it is and to learn new ways that you can come together with others to be Christ's hands and feet on the earth.

SHARE *your* STORY

Open your group with prayer. This should be a brief, simple prayer, in which you invite God to be with you as you meet. You can pray for specific requests at the end of the meeting, or stop momentarily to pray if a particular situation comes up during your discussion.

If you prefer, you could use this collect from the *Book of Common Prayer* (*BCP*, p. 228):

Almighty and merciful God, in your goodness keep us, we pray, from all things that may hurt us, that we, being ready both in mind and body, may accomplish with free hearts those things which belong to your purpose; through Jesus Christ our Lord, who lives and reigns with you and the Holy Spirit, one God, now and for ever. Amen.

Telling our personal stories builds deeper connections among group members. Begin your time together by using the following questions and activities to get people talking:

1. Why do you think people so often feel dissatisfied or even at odds with their own physical bodies? How does our culture encourage us to see our bodies?

2. When have you been impressed by what a body can do? What thoughts or feelings do you experience when you are watching someone perform at a high level in sports, dance, or another physical pursuit? In what sense have they "mastered" their own body?

3. What does it mean to feel "comfortable in your own skin"?

extra NOTES

WATCH *now*

DVD SESSION FOUR

Watch the DVD for this session now. Use the *Notes* space provided below to record any key thoughts, questions, or things you want to remember or follow up on.

HEAR *God's* STORY

READ JOHN 21:11-13

"So Simon Peter climbed back into the boat and dragged the net ashore. It was full of large fish, 153, but even with so many the net was not torn. Jesus said to them, 'Come and have breakfast.' None of the disciples dared ask Him, 'Who are you?' They knew it was the Lord. Jesus came, took the bread and gave it to them, and did the same with the fish."

Use the following questions to guide your discussion of the teaching and stories you just experienced on the DVD as well as the Bible passage below.

1. Picture this scene from Scripture. What might the early morning light look like over the water? What would Peter and the others be feeling, seeing, smelling, or hearing?

2. *Have you ever considered that Jesus thinks about the mundane parts of your life, such as your body's need for rest or for regular meals?

3. *What can you see about the character and care of Christ in this passage?

....

....

....

....

....

....

....

....

....

....

....

....

....

....

....

....

....

....

....

....

....

STUDY

NOTES

THREE USES OF THE BODY. Fr. Charlie listed three ways we can think about our physical bodies. They are:

- *Sacramentally* (Our bodies are temples of the Lord; we should care for them properly.)

- *Sacrificially* (Our bodies, including our gifts and talents, are to be used by God for His purposes.)

- *Corporately* (Our church body is to be unified in order to fulfill God's purposes.)

Which of these three most appeals to you? Which one seems most challenging to understand?

CREATE *a* NEW STORY

As you discover more about God's plan for you as His follower, it will mean change— making the decision to go His way rather than your own. This change doesn't usually happen overnight, but it should happen steadily. By starting with small, simple choices, we begin to change our direction. The Holy Spirit helps us along the way by offering us insights into Scripture, bringing to mind verses we have read at just the right moment, and challenging us to love not only those in our faith community, but those who are still seeking God from afar.

In this section, talk about how you will apply the wisdom you've learned in this session:

4. *This week, did you become aware of ways you can use your body in new or better ways to glorify God? Explain. What steps could you take to better care for your physical body?

5. *In what ways do you use your physical body (your hands, your feet, your voice) to sacrificially share God's love with others?

6. *Think about your small group or broader church community, the corporate body: In what ways is it a living manifestation of Christ's presence? What are some tasks or commitments you can undertake with fellow believers that will bless others and point others to the light of Christ? Why is it so hard to speak the truth in love and holiness?

7. Each of you in the group has different gifts and abilities. And every small group has tasks and roles that need to be done. How could you serve this group—perhaps with hospitality, prayer, organizing an event, researching or studying a topic, worshiping, inviting new people? Have each person share what their gift or passion is, and how they could use it to strengthen and build up the group.

8. Spend some time praying about those you know who might respond to a simple invitation to come to a church service, to join your small group, or even to just have coffee and talk about spiritual matters. Ask the Holy Spirit to bring to mind people you can pray for and invite.

9. *Groups grow closer when they serve together. How could you as a group sacrificially serve someone in need? You may want to visit a shut-in from your church, provide a meal for a family going through difficulty, or give some other practical help to someone in need. If nothing comes to mind, spend some time as a group praying and asking God to show you who needs your help. Have two or three group members organize a serving project for the group, and then—do it!

for **ADDITIONAL STUDY**

Take some time between now and our next meeting to further explore God's Word. Read the Bible passages related to this session's theme on your own, jotting your reflections in a journal or in this study guide. You may even want to use a Bible website or app to look up commentary on these passages. If you like, share what you learn with the group the next time you meet.

READ ROMANS 12:1-2

"Therefore, I urge you, brothers and sisters, in view of God's mercy, to offer your bodies as a living sacrifice, holy and pleasing to God—this is your true and proper worship. Do not conform to the pattern of this world, but be transformed by the renewing of your mind. Then you will be able to test and approve what God's will is— his good, pleasing and perfect will."

Have you ever thought of your body as a "living sacrifice"? As Fr. Charlie pointed out, unlike Christians in other parts of the world or at different times in history, it is highly unlikely that we will face persecution or martyrdom because of our faith. We won't, most likely, be asked to make that ultimate sacrifice for Christ. But we have opportunities, every day, to sacrifice ourselves. Can you name some ways you could "sacrifice your body" in order to glorify God? Perhaps using your hands to serve food to the hungry, your mouth to share the good news of Christ, or your mind to help an unemployed or homeless person find a job or shelter? What are other ways you could offer your body as a "living sacrifice"?

READ ROMANS 12:4-8

"For just as each of us has one body with many members, and these members do not all have the same function, so in Christ we, though many, form one body, and each member belongs to all the others. We have different gifts, according to the grace given to each of us. If

your gift is prophesying, then prophesy in accordance with your faith; if it is serving, then serve; if it is teaching, then teach; if it is to encourage, then give encouragement; if it is giving, then give generously; if it is to lead, do it diligently; if it is to show mercy, do it cheerfully."

As you look around your small group, what gifts and talents do you discern among its members? Between meetings, make a call, send a text or email, or even a hand-written note affirming someone in your group. Tell them how God might have a special purpose in this time and place for their gifts and talents. Commit with one another to be unified as a body of believers and to continue to reflect on what it means, corporately, to be a manifestation of Christ.

extra notes

DAILY DEVOTIONS

The Daily Devotions for this week, found in *The Resurrected Life* companion book, will further explore this week's theme of New Body: Manifesting Jesus. You will discover deeper insights into what it means for us to manifest Christ in our physical bodies and also as a church body. The Daily Devotions are a wonderful way of keeping the spirit of Easter alive in your heart all through the week.

....

....

....

....

....

....

....

....

....

....

....

....

....

....

....

....

NEW COVENANT

Experiencing Resurrection Power

"He saved us, not because of righteous things we had done, but because of his mercy. He saved us through the washing of rebirth and renewal by the Holy Spirit."

TITUS 3:5

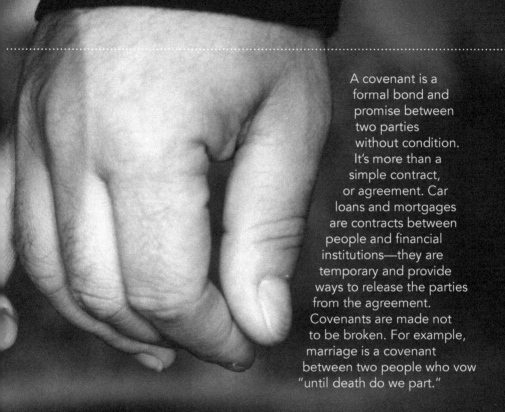

A covenant is a formal bond and promise between two parties without condition. It's more than a simple contract, or agreement. Car loans and mortgages are contracts between people and financial institutions—they are temporary and provide ways to release the parties from the agreement. Covenants are made not to be broken. For example, marriage is a covenant between two people who vow "until death do we part."

Throughout the Bible, God makes covenants with His people. After the flood, He promised Noah that He would never again destroy the earth with a flood. To Abraham, God made a covenant that His descendants would outnumber the stars.

The "new covenant" that we explore this week in *The Resurrected Life* is not made between God and an individual, but between God and all believers. God promises forgiveness and a restored relationship with Himself through Christ's sacrifice and resurrection.

SHARE *your* STORY

Open your group with prayer. This should be a brief, simple prayer, in which you invite God to be with you as you meet. You can pray for specific requests at the end of the meeting, or stop momentarily to pray if a particular situation comes up during your discussion.

Almighty and everlasting God, who in the Paschal mystery established the new covenant of reconciliation: Grant that all who have been reborn into the fellowship of Christ's Body may show forth in their lives what they profess by their faith; through Jesus Christ our Lord, who lives and reigns with you and the Holy Spirit, one God, for ever and ever. Amen. (BCP p. 224)

Telling our personal stories builds deeper connections among group members. Begin your time together by using the following questions and activities to get people talking. Sharing our stories requires us to be honest. We can help one another to be honest and open by creating a safe place; be sure that your group is a place where confidentiality is respected, where there's no such thing as a "stupid question," and where you listen without criticizing one another.

1. What does the word "covenant" mean to you? Do you hear it differently from the words "contract" or "agreement"?

2. What are some of the covenants that you've entered into with other people?

....

....

....

....

....

....

....

....

....

....

....

....

....

....

....

....

....

WATCH *now*

DVD SESSION FIVE

Watch the DVD for this session now. Use the Notes space provided below to record any key thoughts, questions, or things that you want to remember or ask a question about later.

HEAR *God's* STORY

READ LUKE 22:20

"In the same way, after the supper he took the cup, saying, 'This cup is the new covenant in my blood, which is poured out for you.'"

Use the following questions to guide your discussion of the teaching from the DVD and the Bible passage below. Use the facing page to take notes if you like.

1. *The verse above says that the "new covenant" is somehow in Jesus' blood. But what do you think that means? In your own words how do you explain your understanding of the "new covenant" in relationship to Jesus' body and blood? Why do you think Jesus is making the connection of His body and blood to the bread and the wine?

2. How is this "new covenant" different from the "old covenant" between God and His people? What do you think makes it "new"?

3. *The next time you receive the Eucharist, focus on the description of the cup as the new covenant in Jesus' blood "poured out for you." How might you understand those words differently after hearing the teaching this week and thinking about that concept?

NOTES

THE WORD. The Word of God is described by the writer of Hebrews as "alive and active." Like a sword piercing to the core of our being, the Word "judges the thoughts and attitudes of the heart." (Hebrews 4:12) Worshipers in Jesus have their minds renewed and their hearts set on fire by the faithful, Spirit-filled proclamation of the covenant promise and gospel in Jesus Christ.

THE SACRAMENT. A sacrament is an outward and visible sign of an inward and spiritual reality, or grace. The writer of Hebrews invites, "Let us then approach God's throne of grace with confidence, so that we may receive mercy and find grace to help us in our time of need." (Hebrews 4:16) Partaking of the sacrament of Jesus' body and blood mysteriously joins our souls and spirits to His Spirit of Life. Jesus referred to himself as the Bread of Life.

New Covenant worship life rightly sets our hearts on fire and fills us with life and hope in the presence of the Risen Jesus.

CREATE *a* NEW STORY

The Scriptures tell us that, with the New Covenant, God will put new hearts into the people of God! New means change. As we grow in our faith in Christ, we have opportunities to choose to go His way rather than our own. By making these small, simple choices, we begin to change our overall direction. The Holy Spirit helps us along the way, prompting us to choose God's way, convicting us of wrong choices, and filling our hearts with newfound joy and peace.

In this section, talk about how you will apply the wisdom you've learned in this session to your daily life:

1. Can you think of any parts of your family, neighborhood, or community that evoke the image of the Valley of Dry Bones? Places that seem "dead," places without hope and life? In what ways can you endeavor to bring the light of Christ into those places?

2. *Describe a time when you found yourself sitting in church, feeling like a pile of dry bones instead of a vital, living member of the Body of Christ. What happened that restored you? How could you help others when they are feeling parched and lifeless?

3. *When have you felt, spiritually, like your heart has been set on fire? Have you ever had your eyes opened? Do you ever experience that in church? When you are praying or hearing faithful, Spirit-filled teaching of the Scriptures? When you participate in the Communion? Any other times?

4. Spend some time praying about those you know who might respond to a simple invitation to come to church, to join your small group, or even to just have coffee and talk about spiritual matters. Ask the Holy Spirit to bring to mind people you can pray for.

5. A strong group is made up of people who are all being filled up by God, so that they are empowered to love one another. What specific steps will you take this week to connect with God privately, so that He can "fill you up"? If you've focused on prayer in past weeks, maybe you'll want to direct your attention to Scripture this week. If you've been reading God's Word consistently, perhaps you'll want to take it further and try memorizing a verse. Tell the group which practice you plan to try this week, and then, at your next meeting, talk about your progress and challenges.

6. To close your time together, spend some time worshiping God as a group—praying, singing, reading Scripture.

- Have someone suggest a favorite hymn or praise song most people know. Try singing it a cappella, or have someone accompany your singing with a musical instrument.

- Read a passage of Scripture aloud together, making it a time of praise and worship as the words remind you of all God has done for you. Choose a psalm or other favorite verse.

- Ask everyone to share: "How can we pray for you this week?" Be sure to write prayer requests on your *Prayer and Praise Report* on page 144.

- Close your meeting with prayer. This week, you may wish to use this prayer from the *Book of Common Prayer* (BCP, p. 133):

Be present, O merciful God, and protect us through the hours of this night, so that we who are wearied by the changes and chances of this life may rest in your eternal changelessness; through Jesus Christ our Lord. Amen.

for ADDITIONAL STUDY

Take some time between now and our next meeting to get into God's Word. Explore the Bible passages related to this session's theme on your own, recording your reflections in a journal or in this study guide. You may even want to use a Bible website or app to look up commentary on these passages. Ask God to guide your study and give you insight into His Word.

READ PSALM 89:28

"I will maintain my love to him forever, and my covenant with him will never fail."

How has God kept His covenant to you during the course of your life so far? Can you identify people or events that have, in retrospect, seemed like well-timed gifts from God? What do you feel is God's covenant to you in your small group or faith community? What is His promise to you as an individual?

READ 1 CORINTHIANS 10:16

"Is not the cup of thanksgiving for which we give thanks a participation in the blood of Christ? And is not the bread that we break a participation in the body of Christ?"

In his teaching, Fr. Charlie said that sometimes, when we enter the doors of our churches, we might feel like one of the dismembered skeletons in the Valley of Dry Bones. But the moment we hear the Word preached and experience Jesus Christ manifest in the breaking of the bread, in a mysterious and powerful way, we are restored. Have you ever experienced your heart being awakened by the preached Word or at the moment you receive the bread and wine? In what ways is your Sunday worship an experience of the "new covenant"?

Ask God to set your heart on fire and fill you with the life and hope of the new covenant.

DAILY
DEVOTIONS

As you've done in previous weeks, make sure to set aside time each day for the Daily Devotions found in *The Resurrected Life* book. These in-depth reflections will help you stay connected to Christ throughout the week. After the reading, take some time to respond to Him in prayer or in a journal about your personal response to the truths of the Scriptures.

....

....

....

....

....

....

....

....

....

....

....

....

....

....

....

....

....

NEW CREATION

Stewarding the Good News

"Therefore, if anyone is in Christ, the new creation has come: The old has gone, the new is here!

2 CORINTHIANS 5:17

The Bible begins and ends with Creation. In Genesis, God speaks into existence light, land, and all the creatures of the earth, culminating with human beings, made in His image. Adam and Eve are placed in an idyllic garden where they name the animals, walk with God, and, ultimately, disobey. Flip to the back of the Bible and find, in Revelation, the story of God again at work as Creator making a "new heaven and new earth."

Between these two visions of creation we read, over and over again, how human sin causes brokenness and despair. Human sin affects not only our relationships with God and others, but it affects *all* of creation.

This week, we will examine God's original design for creation, how our sin has distorted that plan, and how, together, we can work to renew and restore the communities and world in which we live.

SHARE *your* STORY

Open your group with prayer. This should be a brief, simple prayer, in which you invite God to be with your group as you meet. You can pray for specific requests at the end of the meeting, or stop momentarily to pray if a particular situation comes up during your discussion.

You may wish to use this collect from the *Book of Common Prayer* (BCP, p. 814):

O heavenly Father, who hast filled the world with beauty:
Open our eyes to behold thy gracious hand in all thy works;
that, rejoicing in thy whole creation, we may learn to serve
thee with gladness; for the sake of him through whom all
things were made, thy Son Jesus Christ our Lord. Amen.

Telling our personal stories strengthens the connections among group members. Begin your time together by using the following questions and activities to get people talking. Sharing our stories requires us to be honest. We can help one another to be honest and open by creating a safe place. Be sure your group is one where confidentiality is respected, where there is no such thing as a "stupid question," and where you listen without criticizing one another.

1. When you read that human beings were created "in God's image," what does this mean to you? In what ways do you perceive *yourself* as reflecting God's image?

2. What do you think it means to care for creation?

3. Can you think of examples (from the news, from your life, even from good fiction) where someone's sin wreaks havoc on the natural world?

extra **NOTES**

Creation mandate:
   reflect, reproduce, reign (managers
of creation)
     Paul in book of Romans
     heavenly forces/powers &
     worldly forces/powers will
     be improved. Look at problems
     thru God's eyes.
     God will address problems on
     a micro-level, not a macro-level.
     Example: people who are spiritually
     in tune w/ God will take care
     of their yards/homes

WATCH *now*

DVD SESSION SIX

Watch the DVD for this session now. Use the "Notes" space provided below to record any key thoughts, questions, or things you want to remember or discuss afterward.

HEAR *God's* STORY

READ PSALM 38:8

"I am feeble and utterly crushed;
  I groan in anguish of heart.

All my longings lie open before you, Lord;
  my sighing is not hidden from you.
My heart pounds, my strength fails me;
  even the light has gone from my eyes."

1. What words does the Psalmist use to describe his feelings? Can you think of a time when you felt utterly discouraged about the state of your own life or the world, when everything seemed ruined by violence, inequality, or sadness? What happened?

2. What do you think it means that our "sighing is not hidden" from God? What promise lies beneath the surface of those words?

3. How has human greed or violence damaged the physical creation (nature or animals)?

....

....

....

....

....

....

....

....

....

....

....

....

....

....

....

....

....

....

....

....

STUDY

NOTES

THREE ASPECTS OF CREATION / THE THREE "R'S"

Fr. Charlie lists three aspects of the creation mandate, or, in other words, the plan God had for creation from the beginning. They are for us to:

- *Reflect* God's image,

- *Reproduce* and fill the earth, and

- *Reign* as good stewards over creation.

Fr. Charlie detailed how the Fall distorted all three of these aspects of God's plan for humanity. Because of the world's fall into sin, we witness our sinfulness, as well as dark spiritual forces at work in destroyed natural areas, sectarian violence, and other brokenness in our world. It can be overwhelming. But if we believe Jesus when He says He wants to bring new and abundant life, we can work alongside Him to renew and restore what is damaged in our fallen world.

CREATE *a* NEW STORY

As you begin to more fully understand God's Kingdom and His role for you in it, you will be challenged to change. There will be moments of decision as you begin to choose to go His way rather than your own. By starting with small, simple choices, our entire lives begin to change direction. The Holy Spirit helps us by bringing to mind the things we have studied in the Bible, prompting us to take action, and bringing us comfort in the midst of life's trials.

In this section, talk about how you will apply the wisdom you've learned in this session:

4. *Identify some of the most broken groups of people and ruined natural areas that you can summon to mind. Prisons? Barren, polluted land? Anything close to home? In what ways could you interact with such people and places in order to renew creation?

5. *What are some of the ways you see God in others—or, to put it another way, when do you see people reflecting God's grace, mercy, and love? What might be opportunities for you to serve God's purpose and act as a mirror that reflects God's presence?

6. *What one thing can you do to restore health and spiritual wholeness to your small part of the world? Is there something you could do as a small group together?

7. Finish this sentence: "I can help to restore and renew God's creation by _____."

8. Spend some time praying about those you know that you would like to invite to a church service, ask to join your small group, or just meet for coffee to talk about spiritual matters. Ask the Holy Spirit to bring to mind people you can pray for and look for open doors for invitations.

9. A strong group is made up of people who are all being filled up by God, so that they are empowered to love one another. What specific steps will you take this week to connect with God privately so that He can "fill you up"? If you've focused on Scripture reading in the past weeks, maybe you'll want to spend more concentrated time in prayer. Perhaps you'll want to commit God's Word to memory by memorizing a verse or fast from a specific activity or food. Tell the group which one you plan to try this week, and then, at your next meeting, talk about your progress and challenges.

10. To close your time together, spend some time worshiping God by praying, singing, or reading Scripture aloud.

11. *Invite everyone to share: "How can we pray for you this week?" Be sure to write prayer requests on your *Prayer and Praise Report* on page 144.

12. Close your meeting with prayer.

for ADDITIONAL STUDY

Take some time between now and our next meeting to do some additional study. Explore the Bible passages related to this session's theme and write down your reflections in a journal or in this study guide. Ask God to bring to your mind what you study throughout the week as you need a reminder. If you like, share what you learn with the group the next time you meet.

READ MATTHEW 5:16

"In the same way, let your light shine before others, that they may see your good deeds and glorify your Father in heaven."

What is your role in the renewal and restoration of creation? Are you gifted with people? Are you passionate about protecting the environment? Can you create works of beauty that point to the Creator? Are you an encourager, or talented at listening to those whom others find difficult to love or understand? Ask God how you might play a part in His work to make all things new. Be on the lookout at home, at work, and in your community for people or projects that you could commit to in order to serve as a mirror, reflecting the love of Christ. Let your light shine!

READ MATTHEW 25:34-40

"Then the King will say to those on his right, 'Come, you who are blessed by my Father; take your inheritance, the kingdom prepared for you since the creation of the world. For I was hungry and you gave me something to eat, I was thirsty and you gave me something to drink, I was a stranger and you invited me in, I needed clothes and you clothed me, I was sick and you looked after me, I was in prison and you came to visit me.' Then the righteous will answer him, 'Lord, when did we see you hungry and feed you, or thirsty and give you something to drink? When did we see you

a stranger and invite you in, or needing clothes and clothe you? When did we see you sick or in prison and go to visit you?' The King will reply, 'Truly I tell you, whatever you did for one of the least of these brothers and sisters of mine, you did for me.'"

It's overwhelming to think about all the need and sorrow in the world—to know how many people are naked, thirsty, hungry, sick, or in prison. Some suffer because of sins they have committed; some suffer because of patterns of sin (racism, inequality) that oppress them; others suffer for reasons we may never understand. And, as Fr. Charlie said, when we look at all of the disrepair and need in the world, it can be overwhelming. How can we meet all those needs?

Notice that in Christ's parable of the Sheep and the Goats above, it is never implied that the people who receive the inheritance and whom the King calls "blessed by my Father" were able to help every broken, lonely or marginalized person. That would be humanly impossible. But, each of the righteous ones was rewarded for doing *something.* What one thing can you do to restore health and spiritual wholeness to your world?

DAILY
DEVOTIONS

This week, the Daily Devotions in *The Resurrected Life* book will help you further explore this week's theme of Stewarding the Good News of Jesus Christ. How can you be a more faithful steward of all God has entrusted to you? Be sure to take time for these Daily Devotions. We hope this is becoming a cherished time with God that you don't want to miss!

NEW DAY

Living in the "Now" but "Not Yet"

"This same Jesus, who has been taken from you into heaven, will come back in the same way you have seen him go into heaven."

ACTS 1:11

Every week at church, when we recite the Apostles or Nicene Creed, we affirm both Christ's ascension and His coming again. But how often do we think about what these events mean and how to live in light of the second coming of the Lord?

This week, as we complete our study of *The Resurrected Life*, we will glimpse Christ's ascension—both from the point of view of the eleven Apostles who were present to witness it, as well as from that of the Old Testament prophet Daniel who, amazingly, was given a "sneak preview" of the event.

Before His ascension, Jesus' disciples were eager to see the "Day of the Lord," which they hoped would be a time of abundance and justice for Israel. They asked Jesus: "Lord, are you at this time going to restore the kingdom to Israel?" (Acts 1:6). The disciples wanted vindication and restoration for the nation of Israel. They longed to see Christ's reign established on earth as King of Kings.

When they pressed Jesus for an answer as to when this wonderful day would arrive, they received the answer, "Not yet." Jesus then gives the Apostles their marching orders—they are to bear witness to the Living God to the "ends of the earth." (Acts 1:8)

We still live in this period of "not yet," in terms of the coming of Jesus. We are waiting and longing for his coming again. How do we, in this "not yet" time, bear witness to Christ? This week, as we conclude our study, we will discern how Christ's future return ought to impact us every day of our lives.

SHARE *your* STORY

Open your group with a short, simple prayer. Invite God to be with you as you meet and study His Word. You can pray for specific requests at the end of the meeting or stop momentarily to pray if a particular situation comes up during your discussion.

You may wish to use this prayer from the *Book of Common Prayer*, fitting with the week's theme (BCP, p. 226):

Almighty God, whose blessed Son our Savior Jesus Christ ascended far above all heavens that he might fill all things: Mercifully give us faith to perceive that, according to his promise, he abides with his Church on earth, even to the end of the ages; through Jesus Christ our Lord, who lives and reigns with you and the Holy Spirit, one God, in glory everlasting. Amen.

As we have said in previous lessons, sharing our personal stories builds deeper connections among group members. Your story may be exactly what another person needs to hear to encourage or strengthen them. And your listening to others' stories is an act of love and kindness to them—and could very well help them to grow spiritually. Begin your time together by using the following questions and activities to get people talking:

1.   *What has surprised you most about this group? Where did God meet you, surprise you, or feel most present to you over the last seven weeks?

2.   *What do the parts of the creed that affirm Christ's ascension and future return mean to you? Have you ever given them much thought? Does the Day of the Lord feel urgent and pressing to you, or is it something distant and irrelevant to your life?

3. *Take time in this final session to connect in groups of two or three and discuss: What has God been showing you through these sessions about what it means to live in community? Check in with each other about the progress you have made in your spiritual growth during this study.

4. Take some time for each person to share about how they've done with inviting the people on the *Circles of Life* to church, small group, or out for coffee. What specific conversations are you praying about for the weeks to come?

extra NOTES

WATCH *now*

DVD SESSION SEVEN

Watch the DVD for this session now. Use the *Notes* space below to record any key thoughts, questions, or things you want to remember or follow up later.

HEAR *God's* STORY

READ ACTS 1:9-11

"After he said this, he was taken up before their very eyes, and a cloud hid him from their sight. They were looking intently up into the sky as he was going, when suddenly two men dressed in white stood beside them. 'Men of Galilee,' they said, 'why do you stand here looking into the sky? This same Jesus, who has been taken from you into heaven, will come back in the same way you have seen him go into heaven.'"

Use the following questions to guide your discussion of the teaching you just experienced in the video, and the Bible passage below.

1. Imagine the scene: the Apostles watching Jesus ascend, the empty space where He had stood with them, and then their return home where they had "a prayer meeting." What images come to mind? How might their time of prayer have been different from those we share?

2. *Fr. Charlie affirmed that, after Christ's ascension, He was seated at God's right hand and became "King of Kings" and "Lord of Lords." How are new kings celebrated on earth? What might it have been like in heaven?

3. *How does living between the "now" of Jesus' reign in heaven and the "not yet" of the fullness of Jesus' rule on earth inform your life today?

4. *Is there anything that we can do now to speed or hasten Jesus' return? (See 2 Peter 3:11-13)

....

....

....

....

....

....

....

....

....

....

....

....

....

....

....

....

....

....

....

....

....

STUDY

NOTES

ASCENSION. In the teaching, Fr. Charlie told the story of the prophet Daniel's vision of Christ's ascension and inauguration as "King of Kings:"

"In my vision at night I looked, and there before me was one like a son of man, coming with the clouds of heaven. He approached the Ancient of Days and was led into his presence. He was given authority, glory and sovereign power; all nations and peoples of every language worshiped him. His dominion is an everlasting dominion that will not pass away, and his kingdom is one that will never be destroyed." —Daniel 7:13-14

The prophet had a vision of these events more than 600 years before they occurred.

CHRIST WILL COME AGAIN. We affirm every week at church that we believe in the coming Day of the Lord—that Jesus will return in glory and judgment. So how does the knowledge of and belief in Christ's return affect us, every day?

CREATE *a* NEW STORY

How has God changed your story during this seven-week study? What new things is He asking you to do? What truth has transformed your heart?

Think about specific steps you want to take to live a new story, to walk more closely with God so that you can be a part of His story, engaged in His kingdom.

5. *In the teaching, we heard that each of us is called to a new and abundant life in Christ. In what ways does the work you currently engage in align with the fulfillment of this calling?

6. *Do you ever long for the "no more" that is promised in the New Earth, where there will be *no more* pain, tears, suffering, sorrow, sickness, death, and evil? Does that ever find expression in your prayers as it does in the saints crying in heaven under the altar, "How long, O Lord?"

7. How can you and other members of your small group be more intentional, more mindful of Christ's return? How should the Day of the Lord inform and determine the way you live your life today?

8. As this is the last meeting in this study, take some time to celebrate the work God has done in the lives of group members. Have each person in the group share some step of growth that they have noticed in *another* member. (In other words, no one will talk about themselves. Instead, affirm others in the group.) Make sure that each person gets affirmed and noticed and celebrated—whether the steps they've made are large or small.

9. *If your group still needs to make decisions about continuing to meet after this session, have that discussion now. Consider the third and final study in the Christian Life Trilogy, *The Spirit-Filled Life*. Talk about what you will study, who will lead, and where and when you will meet.

10. Review your *Small Group Agreement* on page 140 and evaluate how well you met your goals. Discuss any changes you want to make as you move forward. If you plan to continue meeting, and your group starts a new study, this is a great time to take on a new role or change the roles of service in your group. What new role will you take on? If you are uncertain, maybe your group members have some ideas for you. Remember you aren't making a lifetime commitment to the new role; it will only be for a few weeks. Maybe someone would like to share a role with you if you don't feel ready to serve solo.

11. Close by praying for your prayer requests and take a couple of minutes to review the praises you have recorded over the past five weeks on the *Prayer and Praise Report* on page 144. Spend some time just worshiping God and thanking Him for all He's done in your group during this study.

DAILY
DEVOTIONS

Continue on your journey through this week's Daily Devotions, found in *The Resurrected Life* book. As you do so, ask God to take you deeper into His Word and help you more fully understand the power and purpose of living *The Resurrected Life.*

....

....

....

....

....

....

....

....

....

....

....

....

....

....

....

....

APPENDICES

FREQUENTLY *asked* QUESTIONS

What do we do on the first night of our group?

Like all fun things in life–have a party! A "get to know you" coffee, dinner, or dessert is a great way to launch a new study. You may want to review the *Small Group Agreement* (page 111) and share the names of a few friends you can invite to join you. But most importantly, have fun before your study time begins.

Where do we find new members for our group?

We encourage you to pray with your group and then brainstorm a list of people from work, church, your neighborhood, your children's school, family, the gym, and so forth. Then have each group member invite several of the people on his or her list.

No matter how you find participants, it's vital that you stay on the lookout for new people to join your group. All groups tend to go through healthy attrition–the result of moves, releasing new leaders, ministry opportunities, and so forth– and if the group gets too small, it could be at risk of shutting down. If you and your group stay open, you'll be amazed at the people God sends your way. The next person just might become a friend for life. You never know!

How long will this group meet?

It's totally up to the group–once you come to the end of this seven-week study. Most groups meet weekly for at least their first seven weeks, but every other week can work as well.

At the end of this study, each group member may decide if he or she wants to continue on for another seven-week study. Some groups launch relationships for years to come, and others are stepping-stones into another group experience. Either way, enjoy the journey.

What if this group is not working for us?

You're not alone! This could be the result of a personality conflict, life-stage difference, geographical distance, level of spiritual maturity, or any number of things. Relax. Pray for God's direction, and at the end of this seven-week study, decide whether to continue with this group or find another. You don't usually buy the first car you look at or marry the first person you date, and the same goes with a group. Don't bail out before the 7 weeks are up–God might have something to teach you. Also, don't run from conflict or prejudge people before you have given them a chance. God is still working in you, too!

How do we handle the childcare needs in our group?

We suggest that you empower the group to openly brainstorm solutions. You may try one option that works for a while and then adjust over time. Our favorite approach is for adults to meet in the living room or dining room and to share the cost of a babysitter (or two) who can be with the kids in a different part of the house. In this way, parents don't have to be away from their children all evening when their children are too young to be left at home. A second option is to use one home for the kids and a second home (close by or a phone call away) for the adults. A third idea is to rotate the responsibility of providing a lesson or care for the children either in the same home or in another home nearby. This can be an incredible blessing for kids. Finally, the most common idea is to decide that you need to have a night to invest in your spiritual lives individually or as a couple and to make your own arrangements for childcare. No matter what decision the group makes, the best approach is to dialogue openly about both the problem and the solution.

SMALL *group* AGREEMENT

OUR PURPOSE:

To talk about what it means to live a God-first life with a few friends.

Group Attendance	To give priority to the group meeting. We will call or email if we will be late or absent. (Completing the *Group Calendar* on page 142 will minimize this issue.)
Safe Environment	To help create a safe place where people can be heard and feel loved.
Respect Differences	To be gentle and gracious toward different spiritual maturity, personal opinions, temperaments, or "imperfections" in fellow group members. We are all works in progress.
Confidentiality	To keep anything that is shared strictly confidential and within the group, and to avoid sharing improper information about those outside the group.
Encouragement for Growth	Accept one another as we are while encouraging one another to grow.
Shared Ownership	To remember that every member is a minister and to ensure that each attender will share a small team role or responsibility over time.
Rotating Hosts / Leaders and Homes	To encourage different people to host the group in their homes, and to rotate the responsibility of facilitating each meeting. (See the *Group Calendar* on page 142.)

OUR *time* TOGETHER

Refreshments/mealtimes will be provided by:

The arrangement for childcare will be:

When we will meet (day of week):

Where we will meet (place):

We will begin at (time):

We will do our best to have some or all of us attend a worship service together. Our primary worship service time will be:

Date of this agreement:

Date we will review this agreement again:

SMALL *group* CALENDAR

DATE	LESSON	HOST HOME	REFRESHMENTS	LEADER
Monday Jan 15	1	Bill	Joe	Bill

MEMORY VERSES

1
SESSION ONE: ALL THINGS NEW
He who was seated on the throne said, "I am making everything new!" Then He said, "Write this down, for these words are trustworthy and true."
(Revelation 21:5)

2
SESSION TWO: NEW LIFE
We were therefore buried with him through baptism into death in order that, just as Christ was raised from the dead through the glory of the Father, we too may live a new life.
(Romans 6:4)

3
SESSION THREE: NEW TEMPLE
Do you not know that your bodies are temples of the Holy Spirit, who is in you, whom you have received from God? You are not your own; you were bought at a price. Therefore honor God with your bodies.
(1 Corinthians 6:19-20)

4
SESSION FOUR: NEW BODY
I eagerly expect and hope that I will in no way be ashamed, but will have sufficient courage so that now as always Christ will be exalted in my body, whether by life or by death.
(Philippians 1:20)

5
SESSION FIVE: NEW COVENANT
He saved us, not because of righteous things we had done, but because of his mercy. He saved us through the washing of rebirth and renewal by the Holy Spirit. (Titus 3:5)

6
SESSION SIX: NEW CREATION
Therefore, if anyone is in Christ, the new creation has come: The old has gone, the new is here!
(2 Corinthians 5:17)

7
SESSION SEVEN: NEW DAY
This same Jesus, who has been taken from you into heaven, will come back in the same way you have seen him go into heaven.
(Acts 1:11)

PRAYER & PRAISE

REPORT

SMALL *group* ROSTER

NAME	ADDRESS	PHONE	EMAIL	MINISTRY	OTHER

SMALL
GROUP
LEADERS

HOSTING *an* OPEN HOUSE

If you're starting a new group, or if this is your first time leading a small group, you should consider planning an "open house" before your first formal group meeting. Even if you only have two to four core members, it's a great way to break the ice and to consider prayerfully who else might be open to join you over the next few weeks. You can also use this kick-off meeting to hand out study guides, spend some time getting to know each other, discuss each person's expectations for the group, and briefly pray for each other.

A simple meal or good desserts always make a kick-off meeting more fun. After people introduce themselves and share how they ended up being at the meeting, have everyone respond to a few icebreaker questions, like: "What is your favorite family vacation?" or "What is one thing you love about your church/our community?" or "What are three things about your life growing up that most people here don't know?" Finally, ask everyone to tell what he or she hopes to get out of the study. You might want to review the *Small Group Agreement* and talk about each person's expectations and priorities.

You can skip this kick-off meeting if your time is limited, but an open house can help set your group up for success.

LEADING *for* THE FIRST TIME

Sweaty palms are a healthy sign.
The Bible says God is gracious to the humble. Remember who is in control. Those who are soft in heart (and sweaty palmed) are those whom God is sure to speak through. God wants to use you exactly as you are to lead your group this week.

Seek support.
Ask your co-leader or a close friend to pray for you and prepare with you before the session. Walking through the study will help you anticipate potentially difficult questions and discussion topics.

Prepare.
Prepare. Prepare. Go through the session several times prior to meeting. If you are using the DVD, watch the teaching segment. Consider writing in a journal or fasting for a day to prepare yourself for what God wants to do.

Ask for feedback so you can grow.
Perhaps in an email or on cards handed out at the study, have everyone write down three things you did well and one thing you could improve. Don't get defensive; instead, show an openness to learn and grow.

Share with your group what God is doing in your heart.
God is searching for those whose hearts are fully His. Share your struggles and your victories. People will relate and your willingness to share will encourage them to do the same.

LEADERSHIP
TRAINING *101*

Congratulations! You have responded to the call to help shepherd Jesus' flock. There are few other tasks in the family of God that surpass the contribution you will be making. As you prepare to lead, whether it is one session or the entire series, here are a few thoughts to keep in mind. We encourage you to read these and review them with each new discussion leader before he or she leads.

1. Remember that you are not alone. God knows everything about you, and He knew that you would be asked to lead your group. Remember that it is common for all good leaders to feel that they are not ready to lead. Moses, Solomon, Jeremiah and Timothy were all reluctant to lead. God promises, "Never will I leave you; never will I forsake you" (Hebrews 13:5). Whether you are leading for one evening, for several weeks, or for a lifetime, you will be blessed as you serve.

2. Don't try to do it alone. Pray right now for God to help you build a healthy leadership team. If you can enlist a co-leader to help you lead the group, you will find your experience to be much richer. This is your chance to involve as many people as you can in building a healthy group. All you have to do is call and ask people to help. You'll probably be surprised at the response.

3. Just be yourself. If you won't be you, who will? God wants you to use your unique gifts and temperament. Don't try to do things exactly like another leader; do them in a way that fits you! Just admit it when you don't have an answer, and apologize when you make a mistake. Your group will love you for it, and you'll sleep better at night!

4. Prepare for your meeting ahead of time. Review the session and the leader's notes, and write down your responses to each question. Pay special attention to exercises that ask group members to do something other than engage in discussion. These exercises will help your group live what the Bible teaches, not just talk about it. Be sure you understand how an exercise works, and bring any necessary supplies (such as paper and pens) to your meeting. If the exercise

employs one of the items in the appendix, be sure to look over that item so you'll know how it works. Finally, review "Outline for Each Session" so you'll remember the purpose of each section in the study.

5. Pray for your group members by name. Before you begin your session, go around the room in your mind and pray for each member by name. You may want to review the prayer list at least once a week. Ask God to use your time together to touch the heart of every person uniquely. Expect God to lead you to whomever He wants you to encourage or challenge in a special way. If you listen, God will surely lead!

6. When you ask a question, be patient. Someone will eventually respond. Sometimes people need a moment or two of silence to think about the question. Keep in mind, if silence doesn't bother you, it won't bother anyone else. After someone responds, affirm the response with a simple "thanks" or "good job." Then ask, "How about somebody else?" or "Would someone who hasn't shared like to add anything?" Be sensitive to new people or reluctant members who aren't ready to say, pray or do anything. If you give them a safe setting, they will blossom over time.

7. Provide transitions between questions. When guiding the discussion, always read aloud the transitional paragraphs and the questions. Ask the group if anyone would like to read the paragraph or Bible passage. Don't call on anyone, but ask for a volunteer, and then be patient until someone begins. Be sure to thank the person who reads aloud.

8. Break up into small groups each week or they won't stay. If your group has more than seven people, we strongly encourage you to have the group gather sometimes in discussion circles of three or four people during the *Hear God's Story* or *Change Your Story* sections of the study. With a greater opportunity to talk in a small circle, people will connect more with the study, apply more quickly what they're learning and ultimately get more out of it. A small circle also encourages a quiet person to participate and tends to minimize the effects of a more vocal or dominant member. It can also help people feel more loved in your group. When you gather again at the end of the section, you can have one person summarize the highlights from each circle. Small circles are also helpful during prayer time. People who are unaccustomed to praying aloud will feel

more comfortable trying it with just two or three others. Also, prayer requests won't take as much time, so circles will have more time to actually pray. When you gather back with the whole group, you can have one person from each circle briefly update everyone on the prayer requests. People are more willing to pray in small circles if they know that the whole group will hear all the prayer requests.

9. Rotate facilitators weekly. At the end of each meeting, ask the group who should lead the following week. Let the group help select your weekly facilitator. You may be perfectly capable of leading each time, but you will help others grow in their faith and gifts if you give them opportunities to lead. You can use the *Small Group Calendar* to fill in the names of all meeting leaders at once if you prefer.

10. One final challenge (for new or first time leaders): Before your first opportunity to lead, look up each of the five passages listed below. Read each one as a devotional exercise to help equip yourself with a shepherd's heart. Trust us on this one. If you do this, you will be more than ready for your first meeting.

> *Matthew 9:36*
> *1 Peter 5:2-4*
> *Psalm 23*
> *Ezekiel 34:11-16*
> *1 Thessalonians 2:7-8, 11-12*

NOTES

NOTES

Artwork Attribution

Page 30 Right panel of the Triptych of Saint John the Baptist and Saint John the Evangelist, 1474-79 (oil on panel), Memling, Hans (c.1433-94) / Groeningemuseum, Bruges, Belgium / © Lukas - Art in Flanders VZW / Bridgeman Images

Page 33 The Incredulity of St. Thomas, 1602-03 (oil on canvas), Caravaggio, Michelangelo Merisi da (1571-1610) / Schloss Sanssouci, Potsdam, Brandenburg, Germany / Bridgeman Images

Page 46 Christ at the Pool of Bethesda, 1667-70 (oil on canvas), Murillo, Bartolome Esteban (1618-82) / National Gallery, London, UK / Bridgeman Images

Page 51 The Appearance of Christ to Mary Magdalene, 1835 (oil on canvas), Ivanov, Aleksandr Andreevich (1806-58) / State Russian Museum, St. Petersburg, Russia / Bridgeman Images

Page 66: The Resurrection: The Angels rolling away the Stone from the Sepulchre, Blake, William (1757-1827) / Victoria & Albert Museum, London, UK / Bridgeman Images

Page 82: Christ at the Sea of Galilee, detail from Episodes from Christ's Passion and Resurrection, reverse surface of Maesta' of Duccio Altarpiece in the Cathedral of Siena, 1308-1311, by Duccio di Buoninsegna (ca 1255 - pre-1319), tempera on wood / De Agostini Picture Library / G.Nimatallah / Bridgeman Images

Page 93 The Supper at Emmaus, 1601 (oil and tempera on canvas), Caravaggio, Michelangelo Merisi da (1571-1610) / National Gallery, London, UK / Bridgeman Images

Page 97: Images Christ on the Road to Emmaus (oil on canvas), Stella, Jacques (1596-1657) / Musee des Beaux-Arts, Nantes, France / Giraudon / Bridgeman Images

Page 98 The Vision of Ezekiel: the Valley of Dry Bones (pencil, w/c & bodycolour with gum arabic on paper), Stanhope, John Roddam Spencer (1829-1908) / Private Collection / Photo © Christie's Images / Bridgeman Images

Page 114 Study for the Resurrection of Christ, 1860 (oil on card), Flandrin, Hippolyte (1809-64) / Louvre, Paris, France / Bridgeman Images

Page 130 Resurrection of the Dead (oil on canvas), Mottez, Victor (1809-97) / Musee des Beaux-Arts, Lille, France / Bridgeman Images

Page 133 Ascension of Christ, by Carlo Bononi, 1590 - 1632, 16th - 17th Century, oil on canvas, Bononi, Carlo (1569-1632) / Mondadori Portfolio/Electa/Antonio Guerra / Bridgeman Images